Contents

Map of the British Isles		Inside Front Cover
1	The Royal Family	p.2
2	Edinburgh	p.4
3	British music	p.6
4	American food	p.8
5	Four English-speaking cities	p.10
6	A festival calendar	p.12
7	English folk heroes	p.14
Map of North America		Inside Back Cover

1 The Royal Family

1 Answer the questions.
   a What do you know about Britain's Royal Family?
   b How many of the British Queen's children and grandchildren can you name?

2 Read the text about the British Queen. Underline facts you didn't know.

The British Queen

Elizabeth II is Britain's current monarch. She became Queen in 1952, at the age of just 25, when her father King George VI died. She reigns (rules) over 16 countries, and is head of the Commonwealth, a group of 54 states with around 2 billion inhabitants. Elizabeth is only the second British monarch to reign for more than 60 years. The other was Queen Victoria, her great-great-grandmother.

Elizabeth got married in 1947 and had four children, Charles (born in 1948), Anne (1950), Andrew (1960), and Edward (1964). She has eight grandchildren, and in 2010 her first great-grandchild was born.

Prince Charles, now in his early sixties, is heir to the throne, which means he will be Britain's next monarch. His two sons, William and Harry, are next in line. The princes' mother, Diana, was Charles's first wife, but they got divorced in 1996. She died a year later in a car accident in Paris. Charles married again in 2005, to Camilla Parker Bowles. In 2011, Prince William also got married, to Kate Middleton. On their marriage they became the Duke and Duchess of Cambridge.

Elizabeth is a popular and successful monarch, but when she was born, nobody thought she would become queen. In fact, her uncle, not her father, was heir to the throne. He became King Edward VIII in January 1936, when his father died. However, love changed British royal history forever. Edward wanted to marry an American woman, Wallis Simpson, who was divorced and a Catholic. The British King couldn't do this, so Edward abdicated: he gave up his position as King, after only 11 months. His younger brother, Elizabeth's father, became King George VI.

Will Elizabeth give up the throne to her son Charles, or will she be Queen until she dies? She is now in her late eighties and is already Britain's oldest monarch. Her husband, Prince Philip, is five years older. Maybe she can continue for many more years. Her mother lived until she was 101 years old!

3 Find these numbers in the text, and write a true sentence for each one.

25 _Elizabeth II was 25 when she became Queen._
   a 16   b 1964
   c late eighties   d five
   e 2010   f 101
   g 2,000,000,000   h eight
   i 11   j 1936

4 Are the sentences true (T) or false (F)?
   1 There are 2 billion people in Britain. _____
   2 Elizabeth is Queen Victoria's great-granddaughter. _____
   3 Prince Charles was born before his mother became Queen. _____
   4 Elizabeth's oldest child is 18 years older than her youngest child. _____
   5 Elizabeth has three sons and one daughter. _____
   6 Camilla Parker Bowles is Prince Charles's second wife. _____
   7 Elizabeth always knew she would be Queen. _____
   8 Elizabeth's uncle died in 1936. _____
   9 Elizabeth's husband is in his nineties. _____
   10 Elizabeth's mother was very old when she died. _____

5 Read the text about royal names.

What's in a name?

Kings and queens rarely use surnames. Everyone knows who they are, so they don't really need them. In fact, royal surnames can become a problem. This is exactly what happened to the British Royal Family around 100 years ago.

For centuries, Europe's kings and queens married people from other royal houses, and all of the families became connected. Often, the marriages helped two countries to stop a war, or become more powerful together. For example, Elizabeth II's husband, Prince Philip, came from the Greek and Danish royal families.

Historically, the British Royal Family was German, and in 1900 its surname was 'Saxe-Coburg and Gotha'. From 1914 to 1918, however, Britain was at war with Germany, and so having a German name was very unpopular. Because of this, Elizabeth's grandfather, King George V, changed the royal surname to 'Windsor' in 1917. Windsor is a town near London, and its castle is one of the Royal Family's homes. Elizabeth II and her descendants – her children and grandchildren – now use this name.

6 Make sentences by matching 1–6 with a–f.

1 Royal families don't use surnames…
2 Many royal houses were connected…
3 Kings and queens married people from other royal families…
4 Elizabeth's grandfather had a foreign surname…
5 The surname was a problem in 1917…
6 Windsor was a good name for the Royal Family to choose…

…because…

a …it was good for their countries.
b …his family came from Germany.
c …they had a home there.
d …they don't need them.
e …they had international marriages.
f …there was a war with Germany.

7 Read the texts again and answer the questions.

Who
1 Who was Elizabeth II's grandfather?
2 Who is the Duchess of Cambridge?
3 Who was Prince Harry's mother?

How many
4 How many states are in the Commonwealth?

Where
5 Where did Princess Diana die?
6 Where is the Queen's husband from?

When
7 When did Elizabeth become Queen?
8 When was Prince Andrew born?
9 When was Edward VIII King?
10 When did the royal surname change?

8 Match the words from the texts with their meanings.

1 monarch	2 throne
3 reign	4 ~~heir~~
5 (un)popular	6 abdicate
7 powerful	8 descendants

a the next person to be king or queen _4_
b strong, able to do many things _____
c the job of being king or queen; the chair where the king or queen sits _____
d (not) liked by people _____
e the people who come after you in your family (children, grandchildren, etc.) _____
f a ruler; king or queen of a country _____
g rule, or have power over, a country _____
h give up being king or queen before you die _____

WHAT DO YOU THINK?

Put the opinions about having a royal family in the correct column.

Royal families are very good for tourism.

Nobody is really interested in the British Royal Family now.

Visits from a reigning monarch are important to help countries to stay connected.

Having a royal family is very expensive. It's not fair that they are very rich, and many people are poor.

Royal families don't live a very easy life.

Traditions like having a royal family are an important part of our culture.

Members of the British Royal Family are very good at their job.

Royal families are no better than ordinary people.

For	Against

Which of the opinions do you agree with?

Does your country have a royal family? If so, how do you feel about them? Compare answers with other students in your class.

PROJECT

Make a poster about royalty in your country. Include these things:

- a family tree of the royal family
- a short description of your current monarch
- royal homes / castles / palaces
- recent royal events, e.g. marriages

If there is no royal family in your country now, research royal history:

- When did your country have a royal or ruling family?
- Who were the most famous monarchs / rulers?
- When and how did royalty end?
- Who rules your country now?

2 Edinburgh

1 What do you know about Scotland's capital city? Think about these things:

A location
B important buildings
C size
D things to see and do

2 Read the texts about Edinburgh quickly. Find a fact for each of headings A–D in exercise 1.

The city

Edinburgh, on the south-east coast, is the capital of Scotland, but not its largest city. Glasgow, around 75 kilometres to the west, has 100,000 more inhabitants, with a population of nearly 600,000. Edinburgh, however, is home to Scotland's most famous festivals and historic sights. Around 1 million people visit it every year. In the UK, only London gets more tourists.

What do they come to see? There are many beautiful buildings. You can see Edinburgh Castle from everywhere in the city, because it sits on top of a giant rock, 100 metres above the city. The current castle is around 500 years old, but there was first a settlement here around 1,500 years ago. There were ancient walls around Edinburgh's Old Town, and so it was very small. To make space for all the people, the houses inside the walls became very tall. In the 18th century, this area was crowded with 80,000 people, but only 20,000 people live there today.

Tourists come to walk The Royal Mile – a long street that runs from Edinburgh Castle to Holyrood Palace, the Queen's home in the city. There are many museums and art galleries, and exciting shops for visitors to explore.

The festivals

Edinburgh is famous for its cultural life. Tourists from all over the (1) _____ come to the city's festivals.

Burns Night – 25th January

This is a celebration of the (2) _____ of Scottish poet, Robert Burns, who lived from 1759 to 1796. People have a special supper of 'haggis' (a Scottish meat dish), sing songs, recite poems, and have a traditional Scottish dance.

Beltane – 30th April

This was an ancient Scottish and Irish festival, to celebrate the start of (3) _____ . In 1988, people started to hold a fire festival in Edinburgh on this day. Now, around 15,000 people go to this festival every year.

Edinburgh Military Tattoo – August

This international celebration of military (4) _____ started in 1950. Every year, hundreds of army bands come to Edinburgh Castle to play. There are 200,000 spectators in the castle, and around 100 million people watch the (5) _____ on TV.

Edinburgh Festival – August

People come to see the 'Edinburgh Festival', but in fact, there are five big events in August. The oldest is the Edinburgh International Festival, which started in 1947 and has theatre and musical events. But the biggest is the Edinburgh Fringe, the world's largest arts festival. There are around 2,000 performers and 250 venues. There is also an international comedy festival, a film festival, and The Edge, a (6) _____ music event. Some festival tickets are expensive, but many of the performances are in the street, and are free for everyone to enjoy.

Hogmanay – December 31st

This New Year's celebration is the first – and last – event in the Edinburgh (7) _____. Over 100,000 people gather in the city's streets to sing, dance, and have a giant party. It's the biggest night of the year. When the clocks strike midnight, everyone stands in a circle and holds hands, to sing 'Auld Lang Syne'. The (8) _____ comes from a poem by Scottish poet Robert Burns, and tells us to remember our friends and our traditions as we celebrate the New Year.

3 Read the Edinburgh city text again. Choose the correct options, A, B, or C.

1 Where is Edinburgh?
   a 75 kilometres from Scotland's coast
   b 75 kilometres east of Glasgow
   c in the west of Scotland

2 How many people live in Edinburgh?
   a 600,000   b 500,000   c 100,000

3 Edinburgh has more…
   a tourists than London.
   b people than Glasgow.
   c tourists than Glasgow.

4 Edinburgh Castle is…
   a 100 metres tall.
   b very easy to see.
   c 1,500 years old.

5 In 18th-century Edinburgh…
   a there was no castle.
   b there were more people in the Old Town than today.
   c there weren't any buildings in the Old Town.

6 What is The Royal Mile?
   a a road
   b a building
   c a museum

4 Read the Edinburgh festivals text. Put the words in the box in the correct places in the text.

| show | summer | song | year |
| pop | music | life | world |

5 Which of the Edinburgh festivals…

1 …is also an Irish festival?
   _____
2 …has army bands in it?
   _____
3 …has a special song?
   _____
4 …do millions of people see on television?
   _____
5 …is about one person?
   _____
6 …happens in Edinburgh Castle?
   _____
7 …has a special food?
   _____
8 …is the biggest arts festival in the world?
   _____
9 …started in the 1980s in the city?
   _____
10 …happen at the same time?
   _____

6 Match the words from the text with the correct meanings.

1 settlement	2 ancient
3 crowded	4 celebrate
5 recite	6 military
7 spectator	8 venue
9 free	10 gather

a with many people   _____
b person who watches a show or event   _____
c place where you can see a show   _____
d with no cost   _____
e do something special for an important event   _____
f come together in one place   _____
g very old   _____
h say or perform a poem   _____
i from the army, or soldiers   _____
j place where people live _____

WHAT DO YOU THINK?

✸ Do you have any festivals in your country which are similar to the ones in the text?

✸ Which of the festivals do you think sound most interesting?
   Burns Night sounds a bit boring.
   I'd like to go to the Edinburgh Festival.
   I don't like military music.

✸ Is New Year's Eve important to you? What do you do to celebrate?
   We always have a big party.
   I spend time with my friends at New Year's Eve.
   It's not a special day for me.

✸ Look again at exercise 1. Write four facts for each heading about the capital city in your country.

PROJECT

Make a poster to advertise your country's capital city to visitors. Include information about:

- location, size, and history
- important buildings
- things to see and do
- festivals (dates and meanings)

Use the texts about Edinburgh to help you.

3 British music

1. What British music groups or singers do you know? Write as many as you can in one minute.

2. Read the text and write the names of places 1–7 on the map below.

THE WORLD'S MUSIC CAPITAL?

Great Britain isn't one of the world's largest countries, but it produces many of the world's top-selling music artists. Music lovers come from all over the world to hear British artists play, or visit places where famous bands started their musical careers. Take a tour of Britain, to find some of its music highlights!

1 London is the capital of England, and the centre of the music scene, too. World-famous rock groups such as Coldplay, Pink Floyd, The Rolling Stones, and Queen all formed in this city. British punk was born here in the 1970s, with bands like The Sex Pistols and The Clash. One of the world's best jazz clubs, Ronnie Scott's, is also in Soho, in central London.

2 Music is a very large part of Irish history and culture. The fiddle (or violin) is an important instrument in most Irish folk bands. There is a long tradition of ceilidhs (/keɪliːz/), or folk dances. Top-selling rock band U2 started in the Irish capital Dublin in the late 1970s, and are still popular today.

3 Around 7.7 million music tourists come to British concerts and festivals every year, spending around £1.4 billion. The Glastonbury Festival is the oldest and biggest event. It started in 1970, when the rock band T Rex performed. For the last weekend of June every year, around 150,000 people come to Worthy Farm in Somerset to enjoy performances by over 3,000 artists, with musical styles from rap to classical. In 2011, these included rock bands U2 and Coldplay, and singers Beyoncé and Cee Lo Green. Every year, Glastonbury Festival raises millions of pounds for charity.

4 People call Wales 'The Land of Song'. Traditionally, people played harps and sang Welsh poems or ballads. Choral singing also became popular here in the 19th century. It started in churches, but large choirs (/kwaɪəz/) often sing at Welsh sports events nowadays. Welsh pop stars are famous for having excellent voices. Successful singers Tom Jones and Shirley Bassey were born in Wales.

5 Liverpool is famous as the home of the world's most successful band, The Beatles. Tourists to the city can stay in the Hard Day's Night Hotel, named after one of the band's songs. Popular attractions include the Cavern Club, where the band played their early concerts. Every August, Liverpool holds the International Beatles Week Festival and the Mathew Street Festival, the largest free music festival in Europe.

6 Scotland is famous for a very unusual musical instrument, the bagpipes. In fact, the pipes come from ancient Egypt and Rome. Nobody is sure when they first came to Scotland, but they were popular by the 17th century. Today, pipers are an important part of traditional weddings, festivals, and sports events. Scotland is also home to many modern musical stars, such as Simple Minds, Franz Ferdinand, and Annie Lennox.

7 Manchester is one of the best places in the UK to go dancing in a nightclub. Electronic house music is a central part of the social scene of the city. Artists from Manchester include pop band Take That, rock group Oasis, and dance music bands The Happy Mondays and New Order.

3 Read the text again and answer the questions.
1. What kind of music do they play at Ronnie Scott's?
2. When did punk start in London?
3. What do people do at a ceilidh?
4. How much money do music tourists spend in the UK every year?
5. How old is the Glastonbury Festival?
6. What are Welsh pop stars famous for?
7. Who sings at sports events in Wales?
8. What is 'A Hard Day's Night'?
9. Where did the bagpipes first come from?
10. If you like dancing to house music, which is a good city to visit?

4 Complete the names of different musical styles from the text. Use a dictionary to check the meanings of words you don't know.
1. p _ _
2. h _ _ _ _
3. d _ _ _ _
4. r _ _ _
5. j _ _ _
6. f _ _ _
7. r _ _
8. c _ _ _ _ _ _ _ _
9. p _ _ _

5 Guess the meaning of these words from their contexts.
1. career
2. highlight
3. scene
4. performance
5. charity
6. ballad
7. choir
8. voice

WHAT DO YOU THINK?

- Which of the musical styles from exercise 4 do you like? Can you name two artists for each style?
- How often do you listen to music? Do you like…
  - …going to concerts and festivals?
  - …listening to CDs at home?
  - …using an MP3 player?
  - …watching music videos on TV or the internet?
  - …listening to the radio?
- Many people take music from the internet without paying. How do you feel about this?

PROJECT

Write an article about the music scene in your country, or a city in your country. Think about these things:
- What musical styles are popular?
- Which bands are the most famous? When did the bands form?
- Who are the famous artists?
- Where are the best places to see bands play?
- What music festivals are there?

4 American food

1 Cover up this page and make a list of foods that you associate with the USA. Write as many as you can in 30 seconds. How many of the foods in the pictures did you think of?

America's top ten dishes

We often think of American food as quick, easy, and tasty, but not very good for us. Many of America's favourite dishes are popular all over the world. But how many of them are actually American? Read and find out!

1 Hot dogs
A hot dog is a boiled pork sausage. They are also called 'wieners' or 'frankfurters' and were originally from Germany (Frankfurt) and Austria (Vienna). The name 'hot dog' comes from 19th-century cartoons, which showed the sausages as talking dachshund dogs. Street vendors started to serve the sausages in a long bread bun so that people could eat them easily at baseball or football games.

2 Pizza
Pizza is a baked flat bread with cheese, tomato, and other toppings, such as meat. Pizzas first became popular around 2,000 years ago in Rome and Greece. People didn't have plates, so they used the flat bread to hold their food. During the Second World War, many American soldiers in Italy tasted pizza for the first time. When they returned home, pizza became much more popular.

3 Milkshakes
The first milkshakes, made around 1885, had alcohol in them. By 1900, however, a milkshake was a drink of milk, blended with fruit or chocolate. Around 30 years later, they also often contained ice cream. In the 1950s, malt shops, which served milkshakes, became very popular with teenagers.

4 Donuts
Donuts (or doughnuts) are round, sweet cakes that are fried and covered in sugar, chocolate, or a similar topping. Originally, donuts came from Europe, and were round cakes with jam in them. An American, Hanson Crockett Gregory, made the first donuts with a hole in the middle in 1847. People often buy donuts with their morning coffee, and American police officers are now famous for always eating them!

5 Pumpkin pie
Pumpkin pie is made from pumpkins, sugar, and spices, baked in a pastry case. Americans traditionally eat this pie with cream or ice cream at Thanksgiving. This festival is on the fourth Thursday in November, and started in the 17th century. Families come together to eat a special meal of roast meat with vegetables, and have pumpkin pie for dessert.

6 Coca Cola
In 1886, pharmacist John Pemberton first mixed a syrup with fizzy water, to make Coca Cola. In the first year of production, Pemberton sold around $5 of the drink, but it cost him $7 to make! Nowadays, you can buy coke in over 200 countries, and every day around 1 billion people drink it.

7 'Subway' sandwiches
Sandwiches were a British invention. They are named after the 4th Earl of Sandwich (1718–1792). He asked his servants to serve him meat between two slices of bread. At first, the founders of 'Subway' called their sandwiches 'submarines', because of their long shape. Now they have more takeaway restaurants than any other fast food company.

8 Tacos
A taco is a fried tortilla (a type of corn bread) served with roast meat, salad, and cheese. The recipe comes from Mexico and is thousands of years old. Nowadays, it's very popular in the Southern United States.

9 Burgers and fries
Although we often call them 'hamburgers', most burgers are actually made of grilled beef, not ham. The name tells us where the food came from: Hamburg in Germany! The burger normally has a round bread bun, salad, and sauces like mustard or ketchup. Most people eat their burgers with French fries – sliced, fried potatoes. The most popular burger is the McDonald's Big Mac. Every day, over 500 million Americans eat one.

10 Chocolate chip cookies
These biscuits are a true American invention. In 1930, a restaurant owner called Ruth Wakefield created them by accident while making cookies. She added chocolate chips, and expected them to melt during cooking, to make a brown cookie. When the chips stayed solid, a great American favourite was born.

2 Where would you expect to eat each of these foods?
  - in the street?
  - at a café or restaurant?
  - with family at home?

3 Which of the foods do you think are:
  - unhealthy?
  - delicious?
  - quick and easy to make?

4 Read the text and write the numbers of the food / drink next to the pictures.

5 Read the text again, and answer the questions.
  1 Which foods or drinks started in other countries?
     _1_ , ___ , ___ , ___ , ___ , ___
  2 Which food or drink was named after a cartoon? ___
  3 Which are the oldest foods? ___ , ___
  4 Which food or drink is the newest? ___
  5 Which food do people eat on a particular date? ___
  6 Which food became more popular because of a war? ___
  7 Who didn't plan to make a popular new food? ___
  8 Which food are Americans famous for eating at sports events? ___
  9 Which food or drink do the most people buy? ___
  10 Which food or drink used to contain alcohol? ___

6 Use the cookery verbs below to label the pictures.

| boil | serve | bake | blend | fry |
| roast | slice | grill | melt | |

a _____ : cook in a lot of hot oil

b _____ : mix together

c _____ : cut thinly

d _____ : cook over or under a hot heat

e _____ : cook in an oven with a little oil

f _____ : cook in water

g _____ : give to someone to eat

h _____ : become soft or liquid when hot

i _____ : cook in an oven

7 Which of the foods in the text can you describe with these adjectives? Use a dictionary to help you.
  1 savoury   _pizza,_ _____
  2 hot and spicy   _____
  3 sweet   _____
  4 salty   _____
  5 crunchy   _____
  6 oily   _____

WHAT DO YOU THINK?

- Which of the American dishes are popular in your country? Do you eat any of them regularly?
- What are the top ten dishes in your country? In groups, make a list. Then discuss your choices as a class.
- Compare your top ten dishes with the American ones. Are there any which are similar?
- How do you cook your top ten dishes? Describe the recipe to a partner, and see if he / she can guess the dish.
- Do some research into the history of some popular food and drink from your country.

PROJECT

Write a website guide to food and drink from your country, with a short description of your top ten dishes. Use the text about the American dishes to help you.

5 Four English-speaking cities

1 Look at the titles of the four city texts. What do you know about these cities? Make notes.

Sydney

Sydney is a beautiful city in south-east Australia. With a population of nearly 5 million, it is Australia's largest city, but it isn't the country's capital. Sydney is a modern city with a short history. The British started to build there when they first came to Australia in 1788. Sydney is on the coast of the Tasman Sea, and its harbour area and beaches are important for trade and tourism. It's a great place to visit for sailing, surfing, arts, and culture. The city has many well-known art galleries and museums, and the design of the Sydney Opera House is world famous. Around 2.7 million international tourists visit the city every year. It's easy to get around by bus, taxi, or on a ferry across the harbour. Shoppers can also use the Metro Monorail trains, which travel around the shopping district and Darling Harbour.

Cape Town

Cape Town is South Africa's second-largest city after Johannesburg, with a population of around 3.5 million. The city has a beautiful location, between the enormous Table Mountain and the Atlantic Ocean. Cape Town is Africa's most popular tourist destination, with around 1.5 million visitors a year. They come to see the fantastic views from the top of Table Mountain, or to enjoy the city's beaches. Not everyone in Cape Town speaks English at home (40 per cent of the population speak Afrikaans), but everyone understands it, and the city is a popular place for students to come and learn English. There was a prison on Robben Island, 10 kilometres from the city, from the 17th to the 20th century. Nelson Mandela was a prisoner there, before he became South Africa's president. Now tourists can visit the island's museum to learn about its history.

Mumbai

Mumbai is on the west coast of India, and is in fact seven islands. Until 1996, people called this city Bombay. It is the fourth-largest city in the world, with a population of around 18 million. It's not surprising that Mumbai is noisy and crowded with people! Fishing, trade by sea, banking, and film-making are important industries, and Mumbai is the richest city in India. The city is very old and has a history of many different rulers. As a result, it's a very cosmopolitan place. Marathi is the official language of Mumbai, but people speak many languages. English is most common for doing business. Tourists come to Mumbai to see its beautiful parks, beaches, and old buildings, but it can also be a dangerous place to visit.

Toronto

Toronto is the largest city in Canada, with a population of around 5 million. There are many international immigrants, and only half of Toronto's inhabitants were born in Canada. Why is the city so popular? It has a lovely location, at the north-west of Lake Ontario, and it is Canada's richest city, an important centre for banking, business, film, and TV. It is quite a new city, only around 220 years old. Toronto's CN (Canadian National) Tower, built in 1976, was the world's tallest building for 34 years. At the top, you can see for up to 120 kilometres, and you can eat your dinner 350 metres above the city in the tower's restaurant. Toronto is an important centre for dance, theatre, and the arts. It also has one of the largest shopping malls in the world, the Eaton Centre. This is Toronto's top attraction, with over 52 million visitors every year. Canada has very cold winters, and so Toronto has PATH, an amazing underground network with shops, restaurants, and other places of interest. You can visit all of the important museums and public buildings, without walking on the streets!

2 Read the texts again. Which city / cities…

1 …aren't very old?
_____
2 …isn't the largest city in its country?
_____
3 …has very cold winters?
_____
4 …has the most people?
_____
5 …is not by the sea / ocean?
_____
6 …has the most tourists?
_____
7 …doesn't have English as its official language?
_____
8 …has the smallest population?
_____
9 …is a popular place for learning English?
_____
10 …changed its name not long ago?
_____

3 Are the sentences true (T) or false (F)?

1 Sydney is around 300 years old. _____
2 You can travel by boat in Sydney. _____
3 Mumbai is a very busy place. _____
4 Mumbai has a short history. _____
5 Cape Town is on a mountain. _____
6 Nelson Mandela was in prison in Cape Town. _____
7 Many people choose to move to Toronto. _____
8 Toronto has the world's tallest building. _____

4 Choose the word with a similar meaning.

visitor	= <u>tourist</u> / immigrant
1 inhabitant	= prisoner / resident
2 get around	= travel / build
3 industry	= business / history
4 amazing	= dangerous / fantastic
5 attraction	= tourist destination / tower
6 beautiful	= rich / lovely
7 well-known	= famous / enormous
8 district	= harbour / area
9 cosmopolitan	= international / underground
10 common	= cold / popular
11 modern	= old / new

5 Complete the sentences with a word from the box.

| immigrants | born | views |
| crowded | everyone | network |

1 There's a big bus _____ , so it's easy to get around.
2 My parents are _____ . They came from India to live in England 20 years ago.
3 The museum is interesting, but it's very _____ . There are thousands of people there!
4 The _____ of the city from the top of this building are great!
5 _____ learns English at school here, from the age of five.
6 My grandfather was _____ in London, but now he lives in Sydney.

WHAT DO YOU THINK?

Which city would you most like to visit? Why?

I'd like to go to Toronto, because I'd like to go up the CN Tower.

I'd like to visit the Sydney Opera House. I think it's an amazing building.

Work in groups of four. Each person in the group chooses one of the cities and writes five questions about it, using the information in the text.

How many people live there?

How old is it?

Where is it?

Give your answers. Guess the city.

PROJECT

Use the internet to research facts about a city that you would like to visit. Find information about:

- location
- population
- language
- transport
- history
- things to see and do

Imagine that you live in the city. Write an email to a friend. Invite him / her to your city. Give some information about the city, and tell your friend about the things he / she can visit. Use words from exercise 4 to help you to describe the city.

6 A festival calendar

1 Read texts A–H quickly and match them to the pictures i–viii.

2 Label the texts with the correct names. Number them in the order they happen in the year (1–8).

Bonfire night	May Day	Christmas
New Year's Eve	Easter	Halloween
Harvest Festival	Valentine's Day	

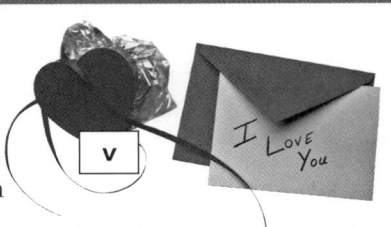

A <u>Bonfire Night (picture iii)</u> – **November 5th**   6
This is an autumn fire festival, and also has the name 'Guy Fawkes' Night'. People light large bonfires and burn models of Guy Fawkes. Afterwards, there is a firework display. In the 16th and 17th centuries, there were religious wars in England. In 1605, Guy Fawkes tried to kill James I, the English King. Guy Fawkes had a lot of gunpowder, and he tried to blow up the Houses of Parliament in London. But soldiers found him before he lit the gunpowder, so he was unsuccessful. Nowadays, we use fire and gunpowder in fireworks to celebrate the King's victory.

B _____ – **May 1st** _____
This is a very old festival, to celebrate the start of summer. Sometimes people stay up all night to see the sun rise on the first morning of May. Morris men, traditional English dancers, wear special clothes with flowers and ribbons. They sing and dance. A pretty young girl becomes the May Queen, and goes on a parade through the streets.

C _____ – **December 25th** _____
This winter festival is perhaps the most important in the UK festival calendar. People decorate their homes with lights, a wreath of plants, and a special tree. They send cards and give presents to friends and family. On the evening of December 24th, children put out stockings (large socks) for Santa. They often leave him some mince pies (special cakes) too. In the morning, the stockings are full of small presents. Traditionally, December 26th was the day of celebration for servants in rich houses. People gave them a small box of food and money, so the day was named Boxing Day.

D _____ – March or April _____

The date of this religious spring festival moves every year, but it is always on a Sunday in March or April. Traditionally, the festival celebrates the story of Jesus Christ dying and coming back to life. Baby animals and eggs are symbols of this new life. Children often paint eggs and decorate special baskets. They are also given chocolate eggs to eat.

E _____ – September/October _____

This autumn festival doesn't have a date. Traditionally, people give thanks for the harvest, or food from the land. Sometimes, they collect food and give it to the poor. In the USA, Thanksgiving has a similar meaning, and is one of the most important festivals of the year.

F _____ – February 14th _____

This late winter festival is a day for lovers. People send cards, poems, and chocolates or flowers to the person they love. Often, the sender is a secret. A typical card has a rhyme like this:

Roses are red
Violets are blue
Sugar is sweet
And so are you.

Love from – guess who?

G _____ – December 31st _____

People go out and have a big party to celebrate the end of the old year, and the start of the new one. At midnight, they share a drink and kiss, then they hold hands and sing a traditional song. People often go to large squares in big cities, and celebrate together. Trafalgar Square in London and Times Square in New York are famous for this. There are often firework displays for the New Year. Scotland is a great place to celebrate 'Hogmanay', as it is called in Scotland, which is the biggest festival of the year.

H _____ – October 31st _____

The name of this festival means 'holy evening'. It marks the start of winter. Traditionally, people thought that the god of the sun went into the land of the dead at this time, and the spirits of the dead came back to the land of the living. People dress in frightening costumes as witches and ghosts, and they make lanterns out of pumpkins. Children go 'trick or treating': they visit their neighbours' houses and ask for sweets. They often tell ghost stories or watch scary films.

---

3 Read the texts again. Write questions for these answers.

1 *Who was Guy Fawkes?*
   He was a man who tried to kill the English King.
2 _____
   She's a pretty young girl.
3 _____
   They put out stockings and mince pies for Santa.
4 _____
   It's on December 26th.
5 _____
   The date is different every year, but it's always a Sunday.
6 _____
   They eat chocolate eggs.
7 _____
   Because they are happy to have good food to eat.
8 _____
   They send cards with a love message.
9 _____
   It's the Scottish name for New Year's Eve.
10 _____
   It means 'holy evening'.

4 Label the Christmas picture with these things.

| decorated tree | wreath | presents |
| Christmas cards | mince pies | stockings |

5 Can you find these things in the other pictures?

| eggs | basket | ribbons | fireworks |
| costumes | flowers |

WHAT DO YOU THINK?

- Do you have all of these festivals in your country?
  How do you celebrate them?
- What do you think of Christmas?
  I always have a special time with my family.
  It's okay, but it costs too much money!

PROJECT

Write a webpage about a festival that you celebrate in your country. Include information about:
- when it happens
- what it means
- the history of the festival
- what people do to celebrate

7 English folk heroes

1. Think about your country's heroes. Were they:
   a kings or queens?   b soldiers?
   c ordinary people?   d real people?
   e legends?

2. Read about three of England's folk heroes. Which of a–e in exercise 1 above are they?

Tintagel Castle

Glastonbury Abbey

England has many legends about folk heroes – good people who fought bravely in wars, and helped others. Most of these stories come from the Middle Ages (12th–15th centuries) and are so old that we can't be sure if they are true.

These are three of England's most famous heroes.

King Arthur

Nobody knows if King Arthur was real. The legend says that he was King of England in the 6th century, but Arthur's story only became popular in the 12th century, 600 years after his death. Arthur's legend says that Arthur was a prince, but his father the King hid him because England was at war. He spent his early years with a poor family. He only became King when he pulled a magic sword, Excalibur, from a stone, at the age of 15. Stories say that Arthur was a good king, and he ruled the land fairly. He had many knights, but he met with them at a round table. The king was not at the top of the table, and this meant that everybody was equal. Many people think that Arthur lived at Tintagel Castle in Cornwall, and that his grave is in Glastonbury, in south-west England. They hope he will return when England needs a true hero.

Saint George

We know that George was a real man, but some of the stories about him are legends. He was born in Turkey in the 3rd century. George had Christian parents, but he became a Roman soldier. The Romans killed many Christians. When George fought against this, they killed him. After his death, the Church made him a saint. A 12th-century story says that George killed a dragon with his spear, and saved a princess. He became the English patron saint, and the English national day, St George's Day, is celebrated every year on April 23rd. George's emblem was a white flag with a red cross. He wore this on his armour and shield when he was in battle. For centuries, English soldiers did the same, because it was easy to see them. This became the English flag. Nowadays, the British flag is red, white, and blue (it is made from the flags of England, Scotland, and Ireland). But you can often still see the red and white English flag today at sports events.

Robin Hood

In the stories, this man had many different names, and nobody knows if he was real. Robin wasn't a king or a knight, but the opposite: a thief! He lived in the forest with a gang of outlaws, his 'merry men'. These included Friar Tuck, a churchman who loved eating and drinking, and Little John, a very big man who was very good at fighting. Robin and his men attacked rich people and took their money. So why were they heroes? Because Robin didn't keep the money for himself: he gave it to the poor. At the time of the stories, England had a very unpopular king. His men took a lot of money from the poor in taxes, and often they were violent with people who couldn't pay. There are many stories of Robin's battles with the king's sheriff in Nottingham, and today Robin is England's most famous folk hero. In the stories, Robin was very good at archery, and in pictures he always has his bow and arrow. There are many books, plays, and films about him. In his home town of Nottingham, they even built a statue of the city's favourite son.

3 Answer the questions about the texts.
1 Was Saint George English?
2 Which part of George's story is a legend?
3 Why did English soldiers wear white and red?
4 What is the difference between the English and British flags?
5 When did the legend of King Arthur become popular?
6 Who was Arthur's father?
7 Do people know where Arthur lived and died?
8 Was Robin Hood a real person?
9 Why did Robin take money from rich people?
10 Where was Robin from?

4 Match the pictures to the words from the texts.

emblem	knight	armour
shield	sword	spear
flag	grave	~~battle~~	bow
arrow	archery	statue

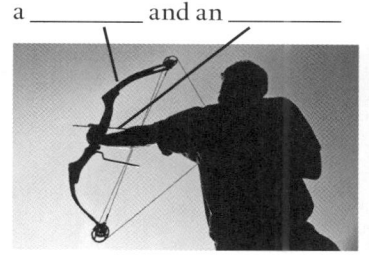

1 fighting a <u>battle</u>  
2 a British _____ 
3 a new _____
4 a man doing _____ 
a _____ and an _____
a _____ a _____
5 a horse with an _____
6 a statue of a _____ 
7 a man carrying a _____ 
8 a _____ of Robin Hood

5 Find the irregular past forms of these verbs in the texts, and write them below.
1 become _____ 2 fight _____
3 wear _____ 4 hide _____
5 spend _____ 6 meet _____
7 mean _____ 8 take _____
9 give _____ 10 build _____

6 Use a dictionary to check the meanings of these adjectives. Which ones do you think are true of the three heroes in the texts?

| brave | talented | rich | young | clever |
| fair | generous | strong | loyal | poor |

WHAT DO YOU THINK?

Do you believe the stories about England's folk heroes? Why / Why not?

I think George was real, but he didn't fight a dragon!

Maybe Robin Hood was a real person, but I don't think he gave all the money to the poor!

Does anything in the stories surprise you?

I'm surprised that George was Turkish.

It's surprising that the story of Arthur started so long after he died.

Which story do you like the best? Why?

I like the story of Robin Hood, because he was an ordinary man, and he helped poor people.

Are any of the stories about your national heroes similar to the texts? How?

Research one of your national heroes.

Answer these questions.
- Is he / she a real person or a legend?
- Was he / she a rich person or an ordinary person?
- What did he / she do to become famous?
- How do people remember him / her (flags, place names, statues, etc.)?
- What is your opinion of him / her?

PROJECT

Write the story of your national hero. Give as much information as you can about your hero's personality and actions, and how people feel about him / her now. Use the texts to help you.

OXFORD
UNIVERSITY PRESS

Great Clarendon Street, Oxford, OX2 6DP, United Kingdom

Oxford University Press is a department of the University of Oxford.
It furthers the University's objective of excellence in research, scholarship,
and education by publishing worldwide. Oxford is a registered trade
mark of Oxford University Press in the UK and in certain other countries

© Oxford University Press 2012

The moral rights of the author have been asserted

First published in 2012
2018
10 9 8 7 6

No unauthorized photocopying

All rights reserved. No part of this publication may be reproduced, stored in a retrieval system, or transmitted, in any form or by any means, without the prior permission in writing of Oxford University Press, or as expressly permitted by law, by licence or under terms agreed with the appropriate reprographics rights organization. Enquiries concerning reproduction outside the scope of the above should be sent to the ELT Rights Department, Oxford University Press, at the address above

You must not circulate this work in any other form and you must impose this same condition on any acquirer

Links to third party websites are provided by Oxford in good faith and for information only. Oxford disclaims any responsibility for the materials contained in any third party website referenced in this work

ISBN: 978 0 19 459832 3

Printed in China

This book is printed on paper from certified and well-managed sources

ACKNOWLEDGEMENTS

The publisher would like to thank the following for their kind permission to reproduce photographs and other copyright material: Oxford University Press pp.2 (The Queen/Corel), 4 (Edinburgh Castle/Digital Vision), 4 (Edinburgh/Digital Vision), 4 (Changing of the Guards/Image Source), 4 (Street performer/Design Pics), 6 (Choir/Digital Vision), 6 (Holstein Cow/Photodisc), 6 (concert/Media Minds), 6 (Beatles waxwork/Corel), 6 (Close-Up of a Violinist/Photodisc), 6 (saxophonist/Photodisc), 6 (Portrait of a Punk Woman/Photodisc), 6 (Man playing bagpipes/White), 6 (Clubbers dancing/Clover), 8 (SubmarineSandwich/Photodisc), 8 (chocolate doughnut/Ingram), 8 (taco shells/Ingram), 8 (Pizza/Foodcollection), 8 (cookie/Photodisc), 8 (glass of cola/Foodcollection), 8 (Pumpkin Pie/Purestock), 8 (Hamburger/Ingram), 8 (strawberry milkshake/Dick Makin), 8 (Hot dog/Stockbyte), 9 (steak and mushrooms/Stockbyte), 9 (Wisk/Fancy), 9 (Tomatoes/Juan Silva), 9 (fish on Barbecue/Image Source), 9 (Roast Turkey/BananaStock), 9 (Pan of boiling potatoes/Edd Westmacott), 9 (couple having dinner/UpperCut), 9 (toddler eating ice cream/Brand X Pictures), 9 (baking/Image Source), 10 (Sydney Harbour/Photodisc), 10 (Cape Town/Peter Adams Photography Ltd), 10 (Toronto Skyline/Photodisc), 10 (Victoria Railway Station india/Digital Vision), 12 (Halloween/Creatas), 12 (Easter Basket/Photodisc), 12 (Fireworks/Thinkstock), 12 (Children at Christmas/Martin Beddall), 12 (Valentine/Photodisc), 12 (Multi-ethnic wedding/Blend Images), 12 (Spanish folk dancer/Photodisc), 12 (vegetables/Ingram), 14 (George & Dragon pub/Corel), 14 (England Fan/Cut and Deal Ltd.), 14 (Tintagel/Corel), 14 (Glastonbury Abbey/Cliverivers), 14 (Robin Hood Inn/Corel), 15 (The 1066 Inn/Corel), 15 (World flags/EyeWire), 15 (Dug Grave/Photodisc), 15 (man shooting arrow/Photodisc), 15 (knights in armour/Corel), 15 (Soldier with Sword/Photodisc), 15 (Goddess statue/Photodisc), 15 (Robin Hood statue/Corel).

Illustrations by: Peter Bull pp inside front cover (Map United Kingdom), inside back cover (Map USA and Canada).